SOLID
STEPPING
STONES

SOLID
STEPPING
STONES

FOR THE
CHRISTIAN JOURNEY

ROBERT P. LIGHTNER

To Ken and Cindy ~ June. 2022

This book has a unique story
behind it. Anne, the publisher, changed
Publishers, offered 340 books To send to
me ~ pay only shipping. It's been a fun
project to give books to many
places, people, and organizations

Love in Christ

Pearl (& Bob in Heaven)
Lightner.

GRACE
ACRES
PRESS

Grace Acres Press
P.O. Box 22
Larkspur, CO 80118
888-700-GRACE (4722)
(303) 681-9995
(303) 681-9996 (fax)
www.GraceAcresPress.com

All Scripture quotations are taken from the *New American Standard Version* unless otherwise indicated. Scripture taken from the NEW AMERICAN STANDARD BIBLE®, Copyright © 1960, 1962, 1963, 1968, 1971, 1972, 1973, 1975, 1977, 1995 by The Lockman Foundation. Used by permission.

Library of Congress Cataloging-in-Publication Data:

Lightner, Robert Paul.
    Solid stepping stones for the Christian journey / by Robert P. Lightner.
        p. cm.
    Includes bibliographical references and index.
    ISBN 978-1-60265-034-3 (pbk.)
    1. Bible. N.T. James--Textbooks. I. Title.
    BS2785.55.L54 2011
    227'.91007--dc22   2011007998

Printed in United States of America
14 13 12 11   01 02 03 04 05 06 07 08 09 10

To Daniel and Natalie Steitz's
adopted daughter,

G I S E L L ,

and foster daughter,

S U R E N I T E E ,

with the prayer that they
will come to faith in Christ
and begin stepping on
the solid stepping stones.

TABLE OF CONTENTS

PROLOGUE

This book is not about how to become a Christian. It is all about how God expects Christians to live out their faith.

The Christian life is begun by a person's acknowledgment that he or she needs a Savior from sin and accepts Jesus Christ's substitution for him or her when He died on the cross.

In the New Testament book that bears his name, Jesus' brother James describes what I am calling "Solid Stepping Stones for the Christian's Journey." These stones have been laid down by God Himself through James, who very likely became a Christian only after his brother Jesus' resurrection from the dead. This book is not a detailed exposition of the book of James. Rather, it is a simplified search for trustworthy footing—solid stepping stones—for the Christian's journey.

The Christian life is described in the Bible with three metaphors. It is a "walk," a "fight," and a "race." Here we are concerned with the walk in the Christian's journey. In both the Old and New Testaments this metaphor is used to describe the Christian life. For example, the Psalmist said, "I shall walk before the LORD in the land of the living"

(Psalm 116:9). Isaiah the prophet wrote, "Come . . . and let us walk in the light of the LORD" (Isaiah 2:5). Paul the apostle told the Roman Christians, "Walk in newness of life" (Romans 6:4). John told his readers to "walk in the light" (1 John 1:7). These are only a few examples; there are many other exhortations to believers to "walk" with the Lord.

Have a blessed trip as you look for "stones" that will be a firm and trustworthy foundation for your walk. I suggest that you not rush ahead nor lag behind, but that you rest in and relish God's provisions for you. I have highlighted a goodly number of "stones" from the many James has laid out for us. You might consider following along in your Bible as we spot these stones. I encourage you to look for other stones as you read. **Don't stumble on them. Step on them.**

MEET JESUS' BROTHER JAMES

(JAMES 1: 1–4)

You and I are going to learn some very exciting things together. The Christian life is exciting, especially when we learn how to walk with God while we discover how He wants us to live and the steps He expects us to take in our Christian journey. First, let's get to know James, the brother of Jesus.

THE MAN JAMES

(James 1:1)

Did you know Jesus grew up in a home where there was rejection and opposition to Him and His ministry? It is true—He did. He was Mary's "firstborn son" (Luke 2:7). She and Joseph, the carpenter, had four other sons later and at least two daughters.

So Jesus had brothers and sisters, but He was the "firstborn," miraculously conceived by the Holy Spirit, as told by Luke the physician (Luke 1:35).

The brother of Jesus we are most interested in here is James.[1] In time, he became the pastor of the church in Jerusalem. However, before he held that prestigious position, and before he wrote the New Testament book that bears his name, he was an unbeliever. He and other members of his family, no doubt his siblings, were offended by Jesus and His ministry (Matthew 13:55, 57–58; Mark 3:31; 6:3).

Think about that for a moment! Jesus, the Healer and Friend of sinners, lived in a divided home. He therefore certainly knew what it meant to have members of His own immediate family oppose, ridicule, and reject Him. We should find encouragement and help if we have had or are having some of the same experiences in our homes. Jesus understands and cares for us no matter what our circumstances are.

We do not know for sure when the members of Jesus' family changed their attitude toward Him. We can be relatively certain, however, that they came to believe on Him sometime after He arose from the dead and before the day of Pentecost. Support for this is found in the fact that Jesus' brothers, Mary, and the eleven disciples were praying together during this time (Acts 1:14). Also, after His resurrection Jesus made a special appearance to James (1 Corinthians 15: 7).

The Lord's brother was recognized as a leader soon after Jesus ascended back to the Father.[2] Also, as noted earlier, James became the head of the church in Jerusalem (Acts 15:13–21). How different this man was from how he responded to Jesus and His ministry earlier! In the Bible book that he wrote, we find him being used mightily for the Lord. Eusebius, an early church father, also tells us that James' knees had grown hard like a camel's knees because of his constant kneeling in prayer.

[1] Six Jameses are named in the New Testament: the son of Zebedee (Mark 1:19), the son of Alphaeus (Mark 3:18), James the less (Mark 15:40), one of Jesus' brothers (Matthew 6:3), the Lord's brother (Galatians 1:19), and the brother of Jude (Jude 1). There is substantial evidence in Scripture that the book of James was written by the Lord's brother. This has also been the traditional view of the church.
[2] See evidence of this in Acts 12:17, 15:13–22, and 21:18–26.

Do we know anything about the death of this brother of Jesus? Not a great deal. But Josephus does record that the high priest Ananus had him stoned sometime after the death of Festus in AD 62 or 63.

The New Testament book of James, written sometime between AD 45–50, is widely acknowledged as the most practical book in the Bible. We might think of it as the book that provides Christians with shoe leather for their daily walk with God. In this book James shows little interest in deep theological issues, unlike the apostle Paul, though he does make some theological statements. James gets down to business with how believers should behave while in the world that they do not believe is their final home.

Recently, a well-known Christian leader was not allowed to enter the assembly hall where a large group of churchmen were to meet. Though this famous leader had every right to attend and had made preliminary arrangements, due to some technicality or administrative mix-up, he was not permitted to enter, because the attendant at the outside entrance gate did not know him. For 30 minutes this well-known Christian leader waited and waited patiently rather than reveal his identity and claim his rights. This example reminds us of James and the way he introduced himself to the friends to whom he wrote.

James does not call attention to himself or to the fact that Jesus is his brother. Instead, he appears to go out of his way *not* to make a point of his earthly relationship with Jesus. He begins his letter by speaking of himself as "a bond-servant of God and of the Lord Jesus Christ" (1:1). In this way he claims no special authority and identifies himself with those he addresses.

A bond-servant in James' day was like a slave in Civil War days. Servants could hire out their services to the highest bidder, but a slave was owned by the master. He was the property of his master and had very few personal rights. He had virtually no will of his own and no work of his own—and therefore, in a sense, little worry of his own.

The position of a slave was not sought after or cherished. In fact, men would do almost anything rather than become slaves. But that is precisely what James said he was of the Lord Jesus Christ.

The full title James gave his Master is very significant: "the Lord Jesus Christ" (1:1). The word "Lord" is a very fitting counterpart to the word "slave." It carries with it the idea of ownership. "Jesus" was the name that identified the Savior with humanity; this was His human name. "Christ" identified Him as the Messiah, the anointed One, promised in the Old Testament. Most of the Jews of Jesus' day denied that He was the promised Deliverer. That is why the religious leaders tried to kill Him before the appointed day of His death on the cross.

THE MESSAGE
(James 1:2–4)

Conservative scholarship largely agrees with A. T. Robertson's view of when the book of James was written: "The Epistle of James was probably written shortly before the Jerusalem Conference, most probably just before, that is A.D. 48 or 49." The practical message of the book was most fitting for the times in which it was written, and it is equally so for our day. Christians of all times need to know what God expects of them and how to walk with God in a world that is opposed to Him and His teaching. There is always the constant need to translate heavenly truths into earthly shoe leather. Children of God must continually be on their guard against becoming so heavenly minded that they are of little earthly good.

It was to "the twelve tribes who are dispersed abroad" (1:1) that James wrote. In other words, he wrote to Jews who had been taken captive and then scattered. They had experienced captivity and scattering from Assyria, Babylon, and Rome. Sometimes they would also migrate on their own to seek their fortunes. However, wherever they went, they always retained their identity and were loyal to their ancient customs. The Jewish historian Josephus said: "There is no city, no tribe, whether Greek or Barbarian in which Jewish law and Jewish customs have not taken root."

Apparently, James used the phrase "the twelve tribes" in a nontechnical or general way. Before James wrote, the ten northern tribes had already disappeared from history. The content of the book reveals that James had a particular group of scattered Jews in mind: those who had come to believe in Jesus as Israel's Messiah. Perhaps James saw and even conversed with some of these Jews as they came to Jerusalem to worship and sensed their need for practical admonition and guidance on their Christian journey.

James calls his readers "Brethren" or its equivalent fourteen times in this small book. This tells us that he wrote to believers who were among the dispersed Jews. His first exhortation to them was, "Consider it all joy . . . when you encounter various trials" (1:2). Next came an explanation of why they needed this exhortation: "the testing of your faith produces endurance" (1:3). An admonition follows: "That you may be perfect and complete, lacking nothing" (1:4).

Did James mean to say that all the trials and trouble that believers experience are joyful? Surely not! What he did mean was that the attitude of our hearts should be joyful regardless of the problems we experience. All our trials and troubles should be viewed in the light of what God knows is best for us in the end. We must never forget that God is always working out His own purposes for us and in us as His children. Trials and testings are God's way of cultivating and strengthening our faith and they produce in us patience. So, it is the outcome in which we are to find our joy, not in the trial itself.

Getting to know James, one of Jesus' brothers, has revealed at least two stepping stones for the Christian journey: humility and a servant mentality. James modeled for his readers, right up front, the need to be humble and to don the role of a servant for Jesus.

Did you find any other stepping stones in this passage?

(1)

(2)

(3)

WISE USE OF WISDOM AND WEALTH

(JAMES 1:5–11)

An old saying goes something like this: "I wish I had been born wealthy instead of so wise, but the fact is I have been cheated out of both wealth and wisdom." I suppose a good number of people feel that way about themselves at times. But the truth is, Christians can be rich in spiritual wisdom and wealth at the same time. The riches of this world, we need to remember, are temporary and cannot buy a lot of things. With the Holy Spirit's guidance, our Lord's brother has given us instruction on how we should view wisdom and wealth.

WISDOM

(James 1:5–8)

At first glance it seems a bit strange that James would call upon his readers to ask God for wisdom after he has just said they should consider themselves blessed and joyful during trials. What does wisdom have to do with our trials? Actually, the two have much to do with each other.

It is heavenly wisdom that we need in order to bear up under the trials and hardships of life.

So, does this mean that all we need to do to be victorious despite hard times is to ask God for wisdom and He will give it? No, there are some conditions attached to what might at first appear to be a blank check from God. First, we need to ask God and He will give us assistance.

The word "ask" (1:6) here means to ask *repeatedly*. It is also used as a request coming from a subordinate and undeserving person. Too, the one seeking wisdom from above is to ask for it "in faith," believing that God will respond positively. There is to be no "doubting" (1:6). Doubters are said to be like "the surf of the sea, driven and tossed by the wind." In other words, God would have us have confidence in Him to do and permit what is best for us. Without this we cannot expect to receive help from God. There is no doubt about it, we all need wisdom from God to know how to view and endure the trials of life. Yet, if we come to Him "double-minded" (1:8), we will be like a person with two souls, like Mr. Face-It-Two-Ways. A person who is double-minded is one with divided allegiance.

The believing Jews to whom James wrote, and by application all Christians since then up to this very day, were called upon to always view trials and hardships God's way. Patience will have an opportunity to do its perfect work only when the child of God uses heavenly wisdom in the face of trials. The tried saint who needs this wisdom is simply to "ask of God" (v. 5). James uses the present tense of the verb, which tells us to keep on asking (cf. Matthew 7:7, where the same usage occurs.). Here, then, is an invitation to persistence in prayer. Wisdom to face life's problems has its source not in the "wise" of this world—Greeks or Jews—but in God.

WEALTH

(James 1:9–11)

The following story is told about the foolishness of putting confidence in money.

A young man said to a millionaire he knew, "You are more to be envied than anyone I know."

"Why is that?" asked the millionaire. "Why should I be envied more than anyone else?"

"You are a very wealthy person," said the young man, "Why, your interest brings you thousands of dollars every month."

"But," said the wealthy man, "all I ever get out of it is my food, clothes, and other necessities of life. I can only eat so much and wear one suit of clothes at a time and lots of people can do that."

"Ah, yes, but think of all the beautiful houses you own and the money you get from all your rentals."

"But I can only live in one house at a time, and the money I get from the rentals I just reinvest in more property. I can't eat or wear the money." After that little interchange the millionaire turned to the young man and said, "I can tell you that the less you desire in this world, the happier you will be. All my money cannot buy a single day more of life for me, cannot buy back my youth, cannot procure me power to keep off the hour of my death, and then what will it all matter, when in a few short years at most I must die and leave all my wealth forever? Young man, you have no cause to envy me."

James plays upon the extremes of poverty and plenty in 1:9–11. In these verses he presents information concerning the way to spiritual riches and then sounds a warning to those who have material riches. These persons face the danger of failing to appreciate the temporary nature of their earthly wealth.

The word "glory" (1:9) forms the link between this section and what James called for in verse 2, "Consider it all joy." In the same way believers are exhorted to find cause for joyfulness in their trials, so those who have little of this world's goods are to "glory" or rejoice in their position in Christ. In both cases believers are the intended audience.

The word "glory" (1:9) may also be translated as "boast." Should those with little of this world's goods boast of their plight? No, but they should boast of their spiritual position in Christ because of His grace.

In God's family, rich and poor are one from His perspective. Neither one has any claim on life. Neither one can postpone the time of death. Both are like the flowering grass and will pass away (1:10). The imagery used here, "the grass and its flower falls off" (1:11) sounds strange to Westerners. We must remember, however, that greenery does not last long, especially not in Palestine. Jesus said of the grass of the field that it "is alive today and tomorrow it is thrown into the furnace" (Matthew 6:30) and used for fuel.

It seems that James was referring to what the prophet Isaiah said: "The grass withers, the flower fades, but the word of our God stands forever" (Isaiah 40:8). The scorching sun soon withers all plant life. After that it is no longer fresh and beautiful. Instead, it is distasteful and very unappealing. James' point is that its beauty is temporary and so is the wealth of the rich. Life on earth is brief and death is sure. Therefore, rich believers should rejoice in their being related to God through faith in Jesus, because that spiritual wealth will endure the test of time.

A Person's Possessions	
From Man	**From God**
Human genius	**Divine wisdom**
Material riches	**Heavenly wisdom**
PASSING	PERMANENT

Let us highlight some of the stepping stones to Christian maturity from James 1:5–11:

(1) Divine wisdom is given so that we may bear up in hard times.

(2) Rejoice in your position in Christ regardless of your financial status.

(3) It is not a sin to be rich or poor. However, our attitude toward either or both can become sinful.

(4) Life is short and death is certain.

Did you find any other stepping stones in this passage?

(1)

(2)

(3)

3

HOW TO PERFORM
UNDER PRESSURE

(JAMES 1:12–17)

Saint Augustine was one of the great fathers of the early church. The story is told that soon after his conversion to Christ he was walking down a street in Milan, Italy, where he was at the time a student. A prostitute saw him and called him by name. "Augustine," she said. He paid no attention to her, though he heard her. She called after him several times, but he did not respond and just kept on walking. Finally she said, "Augustine, it is I." Without slowing down or even looking at her, he said, "Yes, but it is no longer I."

Surely Augustine was enduring temptation at that time. His reply to the prostitute, whom he no doubt knew, indicates his knowledge also of the true source of solicitation to evil and the way of victory as well. Augustine's reply, "It is no longer I," expresses his realization that having become a believer, a Christian, he now had a new enablement to say no to sin and he availed himself of that power. He was a changed man from the inside out.

Our friend James, brother of Jesus, was used of God to give us information about how to have victory over both the trials and troubles of life and the temptations to sin.

ENDURING TRIALS

(James 1:12)

In his original manuscript, James used two different words to set forth God's message about the Christian's trials and temptations. Most English translations show the difference in meaning between these two words and translate the first one as "trials" and the second as "temptations." The context in which these terms are found determines the meanings.

Jesus used the word *dokimos* in 1:3 and 1:12. God allows His children to experience trials and hardships for the purpose of proving the genuineness of our faith. Sometimes we experience fiery trials to purify us and remove the dross in our lives. He wants to refine the pure gold of Christian character in us. God's motives in permitting trials in our walk with Him are always good. Our best interest is always God's purpose.

The word *peirasmos*, translated as "temptation," usually means "a solicitation to evil." This word represents an attempt on the part of someone or something to cause us to sin. Satan, or one or more of his demons, tempts the Christian to sin. God never tempts His children to sin. Eve's encounter with the serpent was clearly a temptation (Genesis 3:1–6). Abraham's experience with God, in contrast, was a trial, a testing (22:1).

The word "blessed" in James 1:12 is used often in the New Testament. When used as it is here, it describes a spiritually prosperous and contented person. James used the word "blessed" here to describe the Christian who has come through a time of trial triumphantly. His spiritual health is good despite the testing of his faith. This person will receive the "crown of life." He has been approved by God and will receive the prize that has been described as "kingly glory." This, of course, is not referring to salvation, but to a reward which often is spoken of as a crown. The Olympics were common in Palestine when James wrote this epistle. He used the imagery of the crown to describe the award from God for emerging triumphant from the testing.

EVALUATING TEMPTATIONS
(James 1:13–17)

"Passing the buck" is a familiar way of blaming someone else for our sinning. This habit is as old as the human race. You may remember that Eve blamed the serpent for her sin when God confronted her. Adam accused Eve for his sin. He even took the matter one step further and, believe it or not, blamed God because He was the One who gave Eve to him (Genesis 3:12).

Today, people still blame God for their sin. You say: How is that done? It is done in a very subtle way. "God made me the way I am and therefore I cannot help myself in some areas." In addition to that, it is often said, "And God loves me as I am," and "God is sovereign and all powerful; therefore He could have kept me from doing what I did, but He chose not to."

James totally rejected such excuses—and so does God, by the way. The brother of Jesus "cut to the chase," probably after hearing some say similar things when they sinned. He made it clear that God is not chargeable for a human's sin, directly or indirectly. He does not entice anyone to sin and He bears no responsibility for it.

If God and others are not responsible for the Christian's sin, then who is? What about the devil? Is he to blame for our sins? No, none of the above is to be blamed for a person's sin. Our friend and brother of Jesus removes every excuse from us for our sin. He puts all the blame upon the sinner. Even though other people and the devil may contribute indirectly, the ultimate cause arises from within the one sinning.

James put it this way: "each one is tempted when he is carried away and enticed by his own lust" (James 1:14). The apostle Paul calls this "the lust of our flesh" (Ephesians 2:3). Christians still have within them some wicked impulses resulting from our inherited sin nature. Yes, Christians are sometimes carried away and enticed by their own lust.

The end result of being enticed or carried away by the lust of the flesh is sin if we do not say no to the evil impulses within us. James illustrates his warning to the Christian by appealing to physical birth (James 1:15). Just as the first thing leading to physical birth is conception, so also the first thing that leads to an overt act of sin is the nurturing of lust or desire.

James appears to make a difference between lust or desire and sin. Desire may be likened to an uninvited impulse to sin. When we do not claim our victory in Christ over sin, the inclination grows and we sin. And then, "when sin is accomplished, it brings forth death" (1:15).

The death that James refers to very likely refers to physical death. God sometimes disciplines His children by taking their lives "prematurely." This is a serious and sad warning. Elsewhere in the Bible this sin is referred to as the "sin leading to death" (cf. 1 John 5:16–17). It is possible for a Christian to come to the place where he or she is no longer useful to God on earth, so He takes that one home.

Some take the death referred to here as spiritual death. This, however, would mean that the believer loses his or her salvation. Such a view would contradict the many passages of Scripture that promise the believer "everlasting life." James' brother Jesus came to give those who receive Him *eternal/everlasting* life (John 3:15–16; 17:2).

As Christians sincerely seek to mature in their faith, James reminds us and admonishes us to avoid several errors. First, we must not imagine that God is responsible in any way for human sin. Though He allows it, nothing evil has its point of origin in God. Whatever comes from God is good (James 1:17) because He is good. Second, we must not imagine that we deserve what God gives us. All that we receive from God is a gift of His grace. Third, everything God allows or does is perfect and purposeful. Fourth, God has been, is now, and always will be, perfect. He also never changes in His divine essence.

God is the Author of light. Any shadow cast by change must therefore come from an earthly source. Yes, shadows from the sun do shift and change, but we must never forget that the One who created the sun does not change.

More stepping stones from James 1:12–17:

(1) Christians are tempted to sin. We must acknowledge this. And we often do, in fact, sin.

(2) Satan has many ways to get us to sin.

(3) God allows trials and testing to come to His children, but He never tempts them to sin.

(4) We must never pass the proverbial buck and blame others when we sin.

(5) We do not deserve anything we get from God. Everything that comes from Him is a gift of His grace.

Did you find any other stepping stones in this passage?

(1)

(2)

(3)

RECEIVING AND REFLECTING SCRIPTURE

(JAMES 1:18–27)

The moon's light is actually reflected sunlight. God made the two lights, "the greater light to govern the day, and the lesser light to govern the night" (Genesis 1:16). The moon receives its light from the sun. Its light is a reflection from the sun. Without that reflection we could not see the moon, only darkness at night.

God's redeemed people have received His Word and are called upon to reflect that Word in their daily lives. Without our reflection of God and His Word, those who do not know Him go on in spiritual darkness.

RECEIVING GOD'S WORD

(James 1:18–21)

Satan not only committed the first sin in the entire universe; he also asked the first question ever asked: "Indeed has God said, You shall not eat from any tree of the garden?" (Genesis 3:1). This is what Satan asked Eve as he began his subtle approach with her.

This question he asked Eve was a subtle attack against the authority of God. Eve was right, God did indeed say that if she ate of the fruit of the tree of the knowledge of good and evil, she would die (Genesis 2:17). Satan contradicted the clear command of God and said, "You surely shall not die" (3:4). From that first rejection of God's word to this very day, God's Word has been ignored, ridiculed, and rejected by many.

Our Lord's brother James, however, entertained no doubt about the Word of truth. He recognized it for what it really is: the means by which sinners are born again and delivered from sin's power in their lives. Today, in our postmodern world where absolute truth is rejected, Christians need to be rightly related to God's Living Word, Christ, and His written Word, the Bible.

Before James challenges his Christian readers to be "doers of the Word," or reflectors of that Word, he reminds them of the great work God did in making them His children. He regenerated them. That is, He gave them new life in Christ. They were born again. They simply received God's gift of salvation. It could not be earned. Rather, they received it by faith in Christ's finished work for them on the cross. God the Holy Spirit bought them, and all His children since then, by the Word of truth. And He did this for a specific purpose.

God's purpose in making us His children is "so that we might be the first fruits among His creation." Here we have a reference to an Old Testament practice. As an act of consecration, and in connection with the Passover Feast celebration, the Jews brought a sampling of the harvest, which was like a token that the rest of the harvest would follow in due time and that it would be the same kind as was represented by the first fruit.

How wonderful of our gracious God to love sinners so much that He devised a plan of salvation for all! But that free gift must be received—accepted—before its benefits are realized. It is a mystery indeed how our sovereign God willed our salvation and by His grace provided it, but still allows us to exercise our will in response to the Spirit's conviction and receive it by faith. The "Word of truth" may be likened to a seed that when planted and watered brings forth the fruit. So the "Word of truth" is that which God uses to bring forth fruit from our lives. We have been made God's children so that we can serve Him by sharing His Word with others.

The opening words of James 1:19—"Know this"—may be taken as a command or as a gentle reminder. The context surrounding these words seems to support viewing it as a command: "Know this." The major point of the passage is that those who receive divine life through God's Word are expected to live by the standards laid down in His written Word. Planting the seed of Scripture in the soil of the soul will result in the kind of fruit described in verses 19 to 21: swift to hear, slow to speak, slow to wrath, and humility ("meekness" in the King James version). People who have truly heard and received God's Word respond to it by putting out of their lives whatever is contrary to that Word.

James has made it very clear that he is addressing Christians because He calls them "brethren" repeatedly (1:2, 9, 16, 19). This helps us understand the kind of salvation or deliverance to which he refers in verse 21, "to save your souls." This refers to the future deliverance of the believer's body from the very presence of sin in the eternal state and not in this life on earth.

REFLECTING GOD'S WORD
(James 1:22–27)

When we look in a mirror, we see reality whether we like it or not. Mirrors reveal facts; they cannot change the facts unless they are intentionally made to distort our images, like the ones at state fair fun houses. Scripture may be likened to a mirror because it too reveals facts: truths about God and humankind's inner being. Apart from Scripture, we would not know the truth about God and about ourselves. Unlike a mirror, God's Word has an inherent power to bring about necessary changes. James talks to us about the effects the Word of truth produces in the Christian's life.

Our Lord's brother has already written about "receiving" the Word. Now he tells us how a person behaves who has had that Word implanted in him. He wants his Christian readers, and all of us by application, to practice these precepts. It is usually easy to listen to instruction and then not to act accordingly. Unfortunately, we are often guilty of doing this, are we not?

It is possible to develop spiritual indigestion. "What does that mean?" you may ask. This spiritual illness comes when we become like a spiritual sponge—taking in the truth but rarely, if ever, giving anything out. The fact is, the more we know by our exposure to Scripture, the more responsible we become to flesh it out with and for others.

To attempt to be a hearer and not a doer of the Word is only to kid oneself. Such a person, James says, is like a person who looks into a mirror and sees things that need immediate attention to avoid embarrassment and then turns his attention to other things and does nothing about what he saw in the mirror. How foolish that would be. The person in James' illustration has taken more than a passing glance at himself. He continues to look. He looks carefully. He is fully aware of his condition but then goes away and pays no attention to what he saw; he does nothing about it.

In contrast to the person in James' first illustration, he also sets forth the person who "looks intently at the perfect law, the law of liberty, and abides by it" (James 1:25). Is it not interesting how James has described God's Word: "the Word of truth" (1:18), "the Word implanted" (1:21), and "the perfect law of liberty" (1:25)?

The perfect law, the law of liberty, at the time James wrote, referred to the Old Testament and the oral teaching of Jesus, his brother. The other books of the New Testament were not yet written when James wrote the book we are looking at now. To be sure, by way of application for us today, the reference is to the entire Bible.

Following through with his illustration of looking into the mirror, James moves on to instruct his readers on how to live out the Word of truth. He has just finished insisting that "hearing" the Word should be followed by "doing" it (1:26). To do the former and not the latter is, to say the least, hypocritical. A specific illustration follows. It concerns the tongue.

Even believers need to bridle—to control—their tongues. "Religious" (James 1:26) refers to outward ritualistic activity. Such things are worthless and useless when the person practicing them does not control his tongue. Our tongues need to be reined in (and James has more to say about the Christian's tongue later on). A Christian with a loose tongue "deceives his own heart." That is, he deceives himself. James was more concerned with right living than he was about religious ritual. There is no doubt about it, the most dangerous beast in all the world has its den just behind our teeth.

The positive characteristics of one who is doing the Word are religious in the proper sense. These are pleasing in God's sight when they are done for His glory. What are these marks? They are doing such things as visiting orphans and widows and keeping oneself unstained by the world (1:27). Such activities, including bridling the tongue (1:26), speak well of God's children and please Him greatly.

Stepping stones from James 1:18–27:

(1) Receiving God's Word.

(2) Reflecting God's Word.

(3) Reading and studying God's Word. It takes time to be holy. We can't be holy in a hurry.

(4) Recognizing that God made the first move in our salvation.

(5) Bridling our tongues.

(6) Reaching out to those in need.

Did you find any other stepping stones in this passage?

(1)

(2)

(3)

5

AVOIDING SNOBBERY

(JAMES 2:1–13)

F our score and seven years ago our fathers brought forth on this continent a new nation conceived in liberty and dedicated to the proposition that all men are created equal." Abraham Lincoln's immortal Gettysburg Address is known and admired by people everywhere. It is true: All humans are created equal before God. However, that really does not mean that there are no differences of privileges, opportunities, abilities, or even capacities among us.

Becoming a Christian does not change a person's IQ or automatically elevate a person from poverty to plenty, from ignorance to intelligence, or from indolence to industry. Nevertheless, as Christians in the family of God we all enjoy a oneness that transcends all social and racial status. Yet, though this is true, Christians even in the early New Testament churches and still today often fail to treat other Christians as brothers and sisters in the family of God. James scolds his Christian readers with strong words for showing respect to some and disrespect to others in the local assembly.

CLASS PREJUDICE

(James 2:1–7)

James has given his readers two basic evidences of a Christian life lived for God's glory: bridling the tongue and reaching out to those in need. He adds another evidence, namely, accepting all who belong to Jesus regardless of their social standing.

Just what is *class prejudice*? Who is guilty of it? James addresses both of these issues. He defines what class prejudice is by giving an illustration, an example of it. Because he introduced the example by calling his readers "brethren," we can be sure to whom he is writing. We have here a sad reminder that Christians are not exempt from showing prejudice and favoritism.

Notice how James describes his brother: "our glorious Lord Jesus Christ" (James 2:1). By associating Him with "glory" and giving His full name, "Lord Jesus Christ," James is giving testimony to Jesus' absolute Deity, which he denied before Jesus died on the cross. The Lord Jesus Christ never displayed any disrespect of persons even though He possessed the fullness of God's glory. It follows therefore that His followers are exhorted against showing partiality.

Very likely, the two men James used in his illustration of prejudice came from the "assembly" (2:2) to which he sent this epistle. Thus, he was touching on something very close to home. The early Christians did not own church property. At first they assembled for worship of Jesus in the Jewish synagogue. Later they met in their homes. All we know about the two men in the illustration is that one was wealthy and the other one was poor.

Whoever was in charge of the assembly or assigned to greet and seat those who came honored the well-dressed, wealthy person and showed disrespect toward and disinterest in the poorly clad one. They did this by ushering the "well-heeled" persons to a prominent and conspicuous seat and those in shabby clothes to what today we would call a back seat. Presumably they were embarrassed about him and did not want him seen any more than absolutely necessary. "You stand over there or sit down by my footstool" (2:3). They really treated the poor person with scorn. By doing what they did, the people in this local assembly or church made themselves judges, and they had evil motives. Both of these things were, and still are, sinful. These are most certainly not stepping stones toward maturity in Christ.

Without asking his readers if they were guilty of this kind of behavior, or why what was done to the two people in the illustration was so wrong, James gave three reasons why such activity was unacceptable to God. First, he made it very clear that God chose to make many poor folks rich in spiritual wealth. He even made them heirs of the kingdom that he promised to those who love Him (2:5).

This means that despising and rejecting people whom God loves is tantamount to despising and rejecting God Himself. Why, God even chose these poor people to be heirs of His kingdom which He promised to all who love Him. The reference here to "kingdom" seems to be a reference to the future reign of Christ on Earth.

Second, the first readers of James' letter were told they had been persecuted by some who were rich (James 2:6). Some of them had even been dragged into court and mistreated by the rich. Why then, James asked, would they dishonor the poor by giving special privileges to the wealthy?

Third, there was no justifiable reason to show prejudice toward the rich who came to their assembly meetings, because some of them could have been known to blaspheme the very One the believer worshipped (2:7). This statement seems to imply that the rich in the illustration may well have been unbelievers. Maybe the leadership of the assembly reasoned that the rich who were treated so well would give to their cause. That always seems to be the motive behind such behavior.

LESSON FROM
THE LAW OF LOVE

(James 2:8–13)

What law did James have in mind when he wrote of "the royal law"? He was referring to the law of love. We know this is so because he quoted from Leviticus 19:18 where it says, "You shall love your neighbor as yourself." His brother Jesus said the same thing in response to a Pharisee's question as to "Which is the greatest commandment in the Law?" (Matthew 22:36). Jesus answered with two commandments. First, "Love the Lord your God with all your heart and with all your soul and with all your mind," which He called "the great and foremost commandment" (Matthew 22:38). He then added a second commandment which He said was like the first one: "You shall love your neighbor as yourself" (v. 39). This is what James said also. James may even have been familiar with what Jesus said on this occasion.

But how are we to understand who is our neighbor? Jesus taught that our *neighbor* is anyone who needs help—rich or poor, young or old (Luke 10:29–37). The lesson to be learned from the law of love, then, is that we must not show prejudice toward those who do not look or believe as we do, nor partiality to those who do. Loving our neighbors, whoever they are or wherever they are, demonstrates that we love as Christ loves us, even though we do not deserve it. We must not think more highly of ourselves than we should.

If we show partiality or prejudice as James describes them here, we sin. We become transgressors of God's law (James 2:9). It seems that James' constituency was quick to recognize the binding nature of God's laws, but slow to apply that truth in their own behavior. To be sure, there were, and there always are, social differences among people. We all have our differences. But the burden of James is that Christians should not allow these differences to make us pander to people in upper social classes. The sin lies in preferential treatment of some believers of recognized social standing, not in the fact of recognizing differences among people.

The law of God is one, just as God Himself is One. Yes, some offenses do have more serious consequences than others. Yet, it is also true that one single infraction makes the one committing it a transgressor "guilty of all" (James 2:10) the law. "How can this be?" the recipients of this letter must have thought.

James answers that query quickly and clearly: "For He who said, 'Do not commit adultery' also said, 'Do not commit murder.' Now if you do not commit adultery, but do commit murder, you have become a transgressor of the law" (2:11).

In the closing verses of James' teaching about avoiding snobbery, he warns of future judgment (2:12–13). He urged his readers to live in light of a coming day of reckoning. Because James' readers were his "brethren," we know the judgment referred to is not the Great White Throne judgment of Revelation 20. At this future judgment, all unbelievers of all time will appear and experience eternal separation from God. Christians (believers) will appear at the Judgment Seat of Christ where He will decide the appropriate reward for their service to Him (2 Corinthians 5:10–13).

The Christian who shows compassion to those who need it, befriends the friendless, comes to the aid of the helpless, and does not demand justice from those who wrong him: that Christian need not dread appearing before the judgment seat of Christ. Our Lord is gracious and will not be harsh or unkind with such a one.

More stepping stones for our journey:

(1) Snobbery is not a stone that we should step on in our journey. It is to be avoided at all cost.

(2) Kindness and respect for others should mark our way.

(3) Jesus never displayed any disrespect for people. We need to follow His example and exhortation.

(4) Let us not judge others, but leave that with the Lord.

(5) Befriend the poor and the rich. God is not a respecter of personal status. Why should we be?

(6) Love others as Jesus loved us.

Did you find any other stepping stones in this passage?

(1)

(2)

(3)

FUNCTIONING FAITH

(JAMES 2:14–26)

Suppose you and some friends were stranded in your car on a cold, snowy winter night. You came upon some very treacherous roads. You drove slowly and very carefully. But in spite of your best efforts, you ended up in a deep snowdrift and you could not get out of it. Fortunately, you did have enough fuel to keep the car running to keep everyone warm until the morning. At daybreak, all of you made your way to the closest house. The man who lived there answered your knock on the door. You explained your plight to him. He extended to you his deepest sympathies and certainly appeared to be very sincere, and you were hoping you would soon find food and shelter. But he offered you and your friends no food and did not even invite you in to get some protection from the bad weather. What he did say was, "I hope you can soon get some help, blessings on you, have a good day."

I suspect that you or I would have serious doubts about the man's concern for us if we had a similar experience. We would likely think, and probably even say, that his talk about our plight was most superficial. What he said was meaningless because it did not include an effort to help us in any way.

Unfortunately, some who profess faith in Jesus and claim to be Christians show no evidence in their lives to support their claim. If, in fact, they have faith, it is not functioning. Our friend James made it very clear that faith without works is dead.

FAITH WITHOUT WORKS
(James 2:14–20)

In Chapter 5, we found stepping stones revealing how our faith should express itself in very practical ways. Perhaps you would like to review these stones. James clearly spelled out how Christians should show Christian love, compassion, and equality in Christ. Now, at this point in our Christian journey, he concentrates on the necessity of doing good works to demonstrate the genuineness of our faith. James' major point is that true faith will express itself in our doing of good works. He argues that there is a mere professed, pretended faith and it is false. There also is a possessed or genuine faith that is accompanied by salvation.

Some folks think that James and Paul were in conflict about salvation. They perceive the apostle Paul as teaching that one becomes rightly related to God by faith and James as teaching that the relationship arises by works. Martin Luther, the great reformer, was so sure that James taught salvation by works that he struck the book of James out of his canon of Scripture. He decided that the two were antagonistic and could not be reconciled, so he opted for Paul and rejected James.

The writings of Paul and James do not contradict each other. Instead, they really complement each other. Their emphasis is different, but they essentially agree. We might put their differences this way: Paul deals with the commencement of the Christian's life and standing before God; James, in contrast, deals with the continuation of the Christian's life and putting faith to work, making it function.

Having stressed the need for Christians to express their faith in the workaday world, James then distinguishes between true or living faith and dead faith. The former is possessed and the latter is merely professed.

To begin, James deals with the problem of a spurious faith by raising thought-provoking questions. In essence, his first question is: What use or profit is there in saying I have faith if there is no corresponding external evidence of that alleged faith? The imaginary person lays claim to be a believer, and may even think he is one, but he gives no evidence of it in his life.

James seems to view that kind of "faith" as mere intellectual assent, an academic nod, a theoretical belief with nothing to back it up. The most important word in James 2:14 is the word "says." Perhaps this person's saying he has faith is because he answered affirmatively to questions like, "Do you believe in Jesus?" "Do you want to go to heaven when you die?" "Do you know that God has a wonderful plan for your life?" It would be hard to find any believer who would not answer "yes" to all these questions, and others in the same vein. James' second question is: Can that kind of faith result in salvation? "Can that faith save him?" The assumption James makes is that if whatever you believe in does not result in a changed life, that kind of faith is "dead" (2:17).

This pronouncement does not mean that a believer can achieve a state of sinlessness in this life. It does mean, though, that the behavior of the believer will correspond to his or her belief. A Christian's conduct complements his or her creed. Real inner faith wears the outward adornment of works acceptable to God—works undertaken, not in order to *become* a Christian, but because one *is* a Christian.

James illustrates his point regarding true faith in the finished work of Jesus and a life which testifies to that. Suppose that someone has a genuine need and you could lend a helping hand, but you refuse to help. Instead, you simply wish them well. What good is that? (2:15–17).

Our friend James sets forth imaginary characters who discuss the relationship of faith and works with regard to salvation (2:18–20). One of these individuals says to the other, "'You have faith and I have works.' Let me see your faith without works and I will show you my faith by my works." These two imaginary persons seem to be saying the very opposite of what James has just said: "faith if it has no works is dead" (2:17). They apparently agree that there are faith Christians and also work Christians. No, there are not two kinds of Christians— one secure in Jesus because of his or her good deeds and another because of his or her "dead" faith. The relationship of faith to works is not an either/or proposition. James does not contend for works without faith any more than Paul contends for faith without works. Both of these men of God were led by the Spirit of God to argue for the work of faith; that is, works that proceed from a living faith. The two— faith and works—are not incompatible. Faith is the cause and works are the effect.

The individual who imagines that he only needs to believe, and that how he lives is inconsequential, is challenged by the one who believes that genuine faith results in good works. He appeals to his friend's belief in monotheism—one true God. He commends him for that true belief. But he reminds the "faith only" man that faith in the existence of one God does not result in salvation. Why, even the demons of hell believe that, though they are surely not rightly related to God (2:19). A final question is asked of the faith-only "foolish fellow": "Are you willing to recognize that faith without works is useless?" (2:20).

FAITH WITH WORKS

(James 2:21–26)

James uses two Scriptural examples to further support his thesis that good works are the necessary product of genuine faith. We will discover that the two Old Testament characters he uses are in some ways opposites.

First, Abraham is introduced to us (James 2:21–24). He was a patriarch chosen by God as head of the nation of Israel. He demonstrated great faith and performed great works for God. If we did not have that context here in James, it would seem what he says about Abraham would conflict with what Paul says in Romans 4:1–3. There Paul declared that if Abraham was justified (declared righteous before God) by works, he could boast in himself. James asks, "Was not Abraham our father justified, declared righteous before men, by works?" (James 2:21). The solution to this seeming contradiction lies in the word "justified" used in both cases. The differing contexts in which Paul and James used the word "justified" must be considered if we are to understand the meaning.

Second, James cites Rahab to further prove that genuine faith results in obedience and good works. This woman was a Gentile and a socially unacceptable sinner. Despite her sinful lifestyle, God stooped to reach her and transform her. By choosing Rahab, James sought to convince his readers of the extent of God's infinite, marvelous, matchless grace.

But this woman lied about the spies (Joshua 2:4–6). How, we think, could God possibly commend her? The truth is that God did not commend her for lying. He commended her for believing in His threat and promise. After all, God had said He would destroy the land and give it to Joshua's men. Rahab took Israel's God at His word. Because of her faith in what He said, she forsook her own people and aligned herself with God's people. In addition, she demonstrated her faith by assisting the two spies sent by Joshua to escape, at the risk of her own life.

Stepping stones for your Christian journey:

(1) Genuine concern for those in need, which concern is demonstrated by helping them.

(2) Understanding that you cannot work for salvation, but realizing that you are called upon to work because you have it.

(3) Do not doubt your salvation because you are not like someone else.

(4) We do not become Christians because we do good things, but because we accept Christ's finished work for us.

(5) Becoming a Christian involves more than believing there is only one God.

Did you find any other stepping stones in this passage?

(1)

(2)

(3)

7

TYING UP
A LOOSE END

(JAMES 3:1-12)

Years ago, a man named Latimer was called upon to preach before King Henry VIII. At the beginning of one of his sermons to the king, Latimer, a godly man, first addressed himself. He said, "Latimer! Latimer! Dost thou remember thou art going to speak before the high and mighty King Henry VIII, before him who has power to command thee to be sent to prison, before him who can have thy head struck off, if it please him? Wilt thou not take care to say nothing that will offend royal ears?" Then, after a short pause of contemplation, he proceeded: "Latimer! Latimer! Dost not thou remember that thou art to speak before the King of kings and Lord of lords, before Him at whose bar Henry VIII will stand, before Him to whom one day thou wilt have to give account thyself? Latimer! Latimer! Be faithful to thy Master and declare all God's Word."

The tongue is the fiercest force in the whole world, and it has its den just behind our teeth. Truly, our tongues must be tamed, be tied up. How different things would be if Christians would always speak as though they were in the physical presence of the Lord Jesus Christ.

As we look at what James said about our tongues, we will discover more stepping stones to Christian maturity.

THE TONGUE HAS TO BE BRIDLED

(James 3:1–4)

Our tongues have to be constantly disciplined. It seems James was concerned that his readers might conclude, from his emphasis on showing our faith by doing, that their tongues have little to do with the Christian life. That certainly is *not* the case. The fact is, our speech is a form of work. Here, then, is another evidence of either a dead faith or a living faith. Early in the Christian era, church services were conducted differently than in our day and time. Men in the gathered group felt free to stand up in the assembly and exhort, teach, pray, sing, or read Scripture. We need to remember that these early Christians met in the Jewish synagogues in the beginning, and they simply followed the way things were done in the synagogues.

Perhaps that way of doing things caused some men to want the position of teacher. They may have wanted more prominence in the assembly. Such was hardly a worthy and God-honoring ambition. James did not want them to take such a position hastily. Neither, of course, did he want to discourage them. So he warned against status-seeking, reminding them that pride and selfishness are sins and that God will judge the guilty Christians at the judgment seat of Christ. Instructing others in the things of God is serious business. No one who is called to do this is perfect: "We all stumble in many ways" (James 3:2). All of us need to bridle our whole body, not just our tongue.

A bridle on a horse is a small piece of equipment, yet it is necessary to control the animal. The same is true of the bit in the horse's mouth.

The bit is a small piece of steel, only about four or five inches long, with holes at each end for attaching leather straps that fasten to the bridle. The bit's purpose is to control the direction of the horse and command its obedience. James' point is that such a small thing as a bit is used to control a large, powerful animal.

Another illustration is the small thing used to guide a large ship: the rudder (3:4). When we see a huge and beautiful seagoing vessel, it is hard to realize that such a small piece of equipment can be used to control the whole ship. Through calm or stormy weather, the rudder makes it possible to direct the vessel where the captain wants it to go.

What the bit is to the horse, the rudder is to the ship. A huge thing like an aircraft carrier and an irrational creature like a horse are both governed by a small thing. But wait: James is going to introduce another small thing that can and often does cause a world of trouble—or can calm a troubled soul.

THE TONGUE'S NASTY BOASTING

(James 3:5–12)

It is almost impossible to miss how James, guided by the Holy Spirit, illustrates his point of small things that have large consequences. First it was the "bridle" (James 3:2), then "bits" (3:3), then a "rudder" (3:4), then the "tongue" (3:5), and finally "a small fire" or spark (3:5).

James returns to the importance of Christians taming their tongues. It sounds as though the people he addressed needed to be reminded how the Psalmist prayed: "Let the words of my mouth and the meditation of my heart be acceptable in Your sight, O LORD, my Rock and my Redeemer" (Psalm 19:14). Today, we too need to ask God to "set a watch upon my lips."

The damage that can be caused by an out-of-control tongue is almost beyond description. Our Lord's brother was led to compare it to a great forest fire that started with a small spark. A careless flip of a cigarette butt can cause, and has caused, fires that destroy hundreds of acres of trees, homes, and lives. The human tongue, yours and mine, can cause irreparable damage as well. The human tongue is "a fire" and a "world of iniquity" that "defiles the entire body and sets on fire the course of our life, and is set on fire by hell" (James 3:6). To put it mildly, the tongue has enormous potential to create both good will and evil.

James continues his description of the evil possibilities of the Christian's tongue. Some of the most ferocious creatures on land or sea or air have been "tamed" by man, yet "no one can tame the tongue" (3:8). That is, in our own strength we cannot tame our tongues. But, by the enablement of the Holy Spirit, we can gain victory over this "restless evil, full of deadly poison."

Think for a moment about the inconsistency of at one moment using one's tongue to praise God and honor Him—and then using it to attack another person made in God's image. How horrible that is, and what a stench that must create before God! Does your faucet at home or the water fountain in the public place give out both fresh and bitter water? No, that does not happen. If it ever did, we would be quick to turn it off and not drink from it again until it had been repaired. Similarly, James gives two more pointed illustrations of our inconsistent use of our tongues. Fig trees do not ever produce olives, not even rarely. Furthermore, the stability of nature keeps salt water from ever producing fresh water (James 3:12).

Take a long, hard look at the simple list that follows. It will remind you of God's view of an evil tongue. Then read the strong stepping stones and place your feet upon them as you live out your faith.

> ### Descriptions of an Evil Tongue
> It is:
> - Offensive, 3:2
> - Small, 3:3–4
> - Influential, 3:3–4
> - Destructive, 3:5
> - Devilish, 3:6, 3:15
> - Insubordinate, 3:7
> - Poisonous, 3:8
> - Inconsistent, 3:11–12

Solid stepping stones for your journey:

(1) Beware of your use of your tongue.

(2) You must bridle your tongue.

(3) Beware of status-seeking and selfishness.

(4) Small things may have large consequences.

(5) Before speaking, remind yourself that you cannot take back what you say.

(6) Claim the power of the Holy Spirit to help you control your tongue.

Did you find any other stepping stones in this passage?

(1)

(2)

(3)

8

MARKS OF
HEAVENLY WISDOM

(JAMES 3:13-18)

C an you imagine it? Socrates, the ancient Greek philosopher, said he did not want to be remembered as one who was "wise" or "a master of wisdom." He believed such a description was true only of God. Socrates preferred to be known simply as a philosopher—one who loved wisdom. We would not expect that, coming from a secular philosopher. What is wisdom, anyway? Is it the same as knowledge? What is the difference between true or genuine wisdom and false wisdom? We will find answer to questions like these in this chapter.

The Old Testament includes three books which together have been called "wisdom literature": the books of Proverbs, Ecclesiastes, and the Song of Solomon, all of which were written by David's son Solomon. David himself said, "Behold, I have magnified and increased wisdom more than all who were over Jerusalem before me; and my mind has observed a wealth of wisdom and knowledge" (Ecclesiastes 1:16). The major theme of the book of Proverbs is wisdom for living.

The important subject of wisdom in the book of James is not a departure from the main theme of James 3. That theme has been how works are evidence of genuine faith (chapter 2). The activity and proper use of the tongue fall into the category of a work accomplished with words (3:1–12). Some among James' original readers were apparently boasting about their wisdom, working their jaws, building themselves up and putting others down in the process. There is a great deal of difference between earthly wisdom and heavenly wisdom. We today need to know the difference just as much as the people to whom James wrote.

EARTHLY WISDOM

(James 3:13–16)

It sounds like there was a lot of bragging going on among James' readers. He begins with a question: "Who among you is wise and understanding?" (James 3:13). There were some who claimed to have both of these admirable qualities. The question distinguishes between wisdom and knowledge. They are not the same. A person can earn several degrees from prestigious institutions and yet not be wise in the use of the knowledge he gained. In the same way, there are those who have very little formal education but show wisdom in the use of the knowledge they do have. In other words, *wisdom* has to do with a person's ability to put to appropriate use the information that he has gained from his acquaintance with the facts.

Those who have been blessed with wisdom do not need to make any announcements to that effect. If we do want to vaunt our wisdom, and do something to make it known in some way, we are at the same time revealing how little wisdom we really have. When one brags about his wisdom and at the same time his behavior contradicts what he claims, he has committed a sin.

Other problems that James' audience had with regard to their "wisdom" were jealousy, selfish ambition, and arrogance (James 3:14). They demonstrated by these sins their total lack of true wisdom or wisdom from above. We could pinpoint the root cause of these sinful traits as the people's total lack of humility. They were an extremely proud people. It has been well said, "A really wise man is a meek, humble man." The person who is meek or humble does not harbor resentment in his heart. He does not demonstrate a spirit of retaliation, and he does not parade his abilities and virtues.

James did not hesitate to call a spade a spade. He was not only specific in his highlighting of his readers' bad behavior, but equally specific about God's view of their earthly wisdom without Him. The wisdom about which some of these folks were boasting was not "that which comes down from above, but is earthly, natural, demonic" (3:15). These are very serious charges against Christians.

Wisdom that does not manifest itself in behavior that is pleasing to God, but instead boasts of its own accomplishments, resents others who are actually more efficient or wise, and displays no true humility, is surely not pleasing to God. Not only that, but such wisdom also fosters schisms and division among God's children and "every other evil thing" (3:16). Paul, the apostle, called such wisdom "fleshly wisdom" (2 Corinthians 1:12). Obviously, such is not the wisdom of God.

Earthly wisdom need not result in behavior that is not pleasing to God, and for many who have it, it does not. The problem is not the wisdom but the misuse of it that causes the attitude and behaviors that displease God. Even those who have both earthly wisdom and heavenly wisdom are often guilty of misusing both, and that is just as sinful.

HEAVENLY WISDOM

(James 3:17–18)

In these two verses (3:17–18), James answers the question he raised in verse 13: "Who among you is wise and understanding?" We gather from what the Lord's brother said between verse 13 and verse 17 that the "wise" person is one who understands the nature and limitation of earthly wisdom. In addition, that person stops bragging about and depending on earthly wisdom. Instead, he or she begins to depend upon "wisdom from above" (3:17). To put it another way, this person becomes more dependent upon God and seeks to please Him. Wisdom from above comes from a study and understanding of God's holy Word. Therefore, it is necessary to be exposed to and to absorb Scripture. It is the only written record about heavenly wisdom that comes directly from God through His chosen penman.

In these closing two verses of James 3 (17 and 18), eight qualities characterize heavenly wisdom and the wonderful consequences of that Godly wisdom. Let us think first about the qualities. If these qualities, these virtues, are true of our disposition, we are viewed by God as wise—not perfect, but wise. These things should mark our attitudes and our actions. If such is not the case, we have only earthly wisdom at that point (if even that).

First, heavenly wisdom is "pure." This word means "consecrated, holy." It implies freedom from what is sensual, earthly, and demonic. To be "pure" is to be free from unworthy and ulterior motives. James' brother Jesus said, "Blessed are the pure in heart" (Matthew 5:8). The one who is pure has had his heart cleansed from sin. His heart is pure before God and so should his head and hands be pure before others.

Second, wisdom from God is "peaceable." Those who have it are not always engaged in agitation over inconsequential things. They do not look for something to argue about. Instead, they seek unity and reconciliation. They want to preserve peace and do their best not to stir up trouble. This does not mean we need to agree with everyone about everything. Rather, the peaceable person holds his position graciously and sometimes simply agrees to disagree.

Third, the wise Christian is "gentle." The original word used here includes many things. Some of these nuances are *reasonable, courteous, kind, gracious,* and *forgiving.* This quality of gentleness tempers justice with mercy and tolerates the limitations of others. It goes the "second mile," as the saying puts it.

Fourth, a truly wise person is "reasonable." The King James version translates the word as "easy to be entreated" (James 3:17, KJV). This spiritual quality means the person is not conceited; does not claim to have all the answers to everything; is not obstinate, unyielding, or stubborn. This quality makes a person easily persuaded to do what is right.

Fifth, those who have wisdom from above are "full of mercy and good fruits." They show sympathy and are quick to come to the aid of those in need. Compassion flows from them toward those who suffer, whether they have their troubles because of their own fault or for some unexplainable reason or unknown source.

Sixth, God's wisdom as displayed by the Christian is "unwavering." This means those who possess this quality are not wishy-washy. They are steady and maintain an even keel. They do not play favorites.

Seventh, God's wisdom makes us "without hypocrisy." The person who has this quality does not play-act. No, this one is free from sham and pretense. Instead, she is sincere, upright, and absolutely honest with herself and others.

Eighth, the Christian who sows peace will reap the fruit of righteousness and will become a peacemaker. Heavenly wisdom yields right conduct and shows forth a peaceful demeanor.

A good conclusion for James' discussion of these marks of heavenly wisdom is to see how they contrast with natural (earthly) wisdom.

Characteristics of Wisdom	
From Man	From God
Boastful	Modest
Resentful	Submissive
Ambitious	Dependent
Jealous	Holy
Untruthful	Tranquil
Divisive	Courteous
Selfish	Pitying, merciful
Demonic	Impartial
Seditious	Sincere

Solid stepping stones for the journey:

The sins under "Natural Wisdom" (listed earlier) are obviously to be avoided. They are qualities that often characterize the non-Christian and are often displayed by Christians also. The qualities under "Divine Wisdom" are really solid stepping stones to Christian maturity. By God's enabling strength and marvelous grace, we need to land on these stepping stones regularly.

Did you find any other stepping stones in this passage?

(1)

(2)

(3)

9

SELF-CENTERED CHRISTIANS

(JAMES 4:1–10)

War among men and nations has been an ongoing enterprise since the dawn of human history. Rather than being an unusual and rare phenomenon, war has been and still is a perennial reality. Feuds between blood relatives also abound and continue—sad but true.

We may ask, "What about conflict between brothers and sisters in the local church and the family of God at large?" Unfortunately, there is a lot of fighting in this arena as well. James, our Lord's brother, knew very well that there was some warfare going on among those Christian Jews to whom he wrote. He did not ask if they had quarrels and conflicts; he knew they had them. Rather, he asked them bluntly, "What is the source of these among you?"

He did not waste any time before telling them what the causes contributing to their conflict were. After that, he told them how to claim the victory over their sinful behavior.

CONTRIBUTING CAUSES OF CONFLICTS

(James 4:1–4)

The contrast between the closing words of James 3 and the opening of chapter 4 is striking. It is between peace-making and quarrels and conflicts. The latter have their source in personal pleasures. To put it clearly, what we have here is a glaring example of Christians giving in to their sinful nature. Becoming a Christian does not result in sinlessness.

We all still have the sin nature that we inherited from our parents, and they from theirs, all the way back to Adam and Eve, who got a sin nature because they disobeyed God and ate of the forbidden fruit. We all still have depraved appetites, and will continue to have them until we die. Even the apostle Paul experienced the struggle between the old sinful nature (or capacity and tendency) and the new nature. He confessed that "the good that I want, I do not do, but I practice the very evil that I do not want" (Romans 7:19).

It sounds like both James and Paul are talking about conflicts and struggles that Christians have. Christians have a perfect standing before God, but no one is yet perfect in this life. Christians still "lust" at times. The word "lust" refers to passions or pleasures. This word is used only three other times in the entire New Testament, and each time it is in a bad or negative sense. James told his readers that their pleasures derive from their fleshly desires, their old sin nature.

Having traced the readers' quarrels and conflicts to humans' indwelling sin nature, James got even more specific, even though his readers were believers (they were Christians). Notice the sinful activities that James called out as characterizing these people: "You lust and do not have; so you commit murder. And you are envious and cannot obtain; so you fight and quarrel. You do not have because you do not ask. You ask and do not receive, because you ask with wrong motives, so that you may spend *it* on your pleasures" (James 4:2–3).

Was James saying that these Jewish Christians were literally committing murder, they were killing each other? I think not. The word translated *murder* or *killing* here suggests destroying not someone's physical life but destroying each other's character or testimony. Jesus Himself said that disparaging the reputation of others and acting in anger toward others were tantamount to murder (Matthew 5:21–22). John the apostle says essentially the same thing (1 John 3:15). The sin James was referring to is as deadly as murder. Of course, the potential for even literal murder persists in the fallen nature of Christians. Even David, the man after God's own heart, never dreamed he would do such a thing. Yet, in a very real sense he did just that by arranging for the death of Bathsheba's husband (2 Samuel 11).

This would be a good time to remind ourselves that James addressed his letter "to the twelve tribes who are dispersed abroad" (James 1:1). This meant it was for all Jewish Christians everywhere. At the early date of James' book, Christians were most likely still meeting in the Jewish synagogues.

The lure of the world was already attracting some of the early Christians. Therefore, there were divided allegiances among them. This was another reason contributing to the conflicts among them. Strong language is used to set forth James' warning to these people. He called them "adulteresses" (3:4). Was he against women? Were not some men guilty of the same sin? No, he was not singling out women. Yes, men were not and are not guiltless of the same sins. The feminine gender was used here, most likely, because the bride of Christ, the church, is feminine and any infidelity committed by Christian men and women is spiritual adultery. When Christians embrace the philosophy of the world and pursue the goals of the world, they have sided with the world and therefore are against Christ.

The term "world" comes from the Greek word signifying the order of things in which we live. It refers to the social, political, cultural, economic, and even religious systems operating at any particular time. The world is that organized system which is headed by Satan himself and leaves God out completely. Little wonder, then, that love of, or dedication to, Satan's philosophy of life is enmity against God. Such divided loyalty on the part of some is certain to cause divisions among God's people.

CLAIMING THE CONQUEST
(James 4:5–10)

Typical of James, he usually supplies the "how to" after a challenging presentation of the problem. In this section Jesus' brother makes it clear that sheer human effort will not bring Christians into conformity with God's desires for them. To put it another way, the spiritual requires spiritual—that is, divine—enablement. And that enablement is available only through the ministries of the Holy Spirit.

The question in James 4:5, "[D]o you think that the Scripture speaks to no purpose?," is quickly answered. James' readers apparently had forgotten that the Holy Spirit of God had taken up residence in them, indwelling each one of them. One of His ministries is that He jealously desires or yearns over God's people. The Spirit broods over the Christian with a mother-like love and with longing to see God's children grow and develop. To put it in the words of the theme of this book, our heavenly Father longs for His children to step on the solid stones He has provided for us as we walk through the muck and mire of the world.

God not only gives the Christian the Holy Spirit of grace, but also gives "greater grace" (4:6) for the Christian journey. He provides grace and strength to "submit" to God and to "resist" the devil (4:7).

How wonderful it is to know that our God is not unapproachable! As the Christian draws near to Him, He in turn draws near to the Christian (3:8). What a wonderful promise and ministry that is!

In the Old Testament, "clean hands" often signified moral purity. Of course, we need to remember that clean hands mean very little if the heart is impure and unclean. The stepping stone marked "cleanse your hands" is very close to the stone marked "purify your hearts" (4:8). If one or the other of these is neglected or unused, the result is double-mindedness which results in divided loyalties.

"Be afflicted or miserable and mourn" (4:9) was James' way of telling his readers to view their sins with the proper attitude. He was not by this exhortation saying that Christians should become morbid, melancholy, and depressed. Perhaps James was thinking how Jesus pronounced a benediction upon those who mourned because of their sin (Matthew 5:4). All of us as Christians need to have a truly sorrowful and repentant disposition when we offend God (as we surely will at some time).

Notice how many responsibilities James puts before the Christian in verses 7-10. There are ten things in these verses that God will not do for Christians. Each of us is called upon to do them. As noted earlier, though, we cannot do these things in our own strength. But we can do them in and through the power of the Holy Spirit.

The final human responsibility James mentions is absolutely foundational for all the others in the list. Pride is truly the crux of the problem. Self-centeredness is the plague of the Christian life. It certainly is not a stepping stone that we should rely on. The problem of cantankerous Christians will be resolved only to the extent that Christians cast themselves upon the Lord and do what the old hymn, "When I Survey the Wondrous Cross," says: "Pour contempt on all our pride"!

There are a lot of solid stepping stones for our Christian journey in this section of James 4:1-10. From these we can find much help for the journey.

Help for the Journey	
Divine Resources	Human Responsibilities
Indwelling Holy Spirit	Submit to God
More grace	Resist the devil
God's nearness	Draw near to God
	Clean your hands
	Purify your hearts
	Be miserable (about sin)
	Mourn over sin
	Weep (over sin)
	Change
	Be humble

Did you find any other stepping stones in this passage?

(1)

(2)

(3)

10

PRACTICAL ATHEISM

(JAMES 4:11–17)

W hat is meant by *atheism*? It is the belief system that says there is no personal God. *Theism*, therefore, describes the belief system which affirms that there is a personal Being the Bible describes as God.

For this chapter, we need to define a third term also. What is *practical atheism*? This refers to a belief in the personal God of the Bible that does not give Him the prominent place He wants in the believer's life. A practical atheist puts God on the shelf, as it were, as people do who worship gods of wood and stone. The truth is, a Sunday-only God, or one to be taken off the shelf only in an emergency, is certainly not the God of the Bible.

It seems rather clear that James faulted his believing readers for being what I am calling practical atheists because of the way they lived. Let's look for some stepping stones to help us avoid behaving as though God does not exist.

SINNING AGAINST GOD'S WORD

(James 4:11–12)

James has already had a great deal to say about the sins of the tongue. We have noted, in Chapter 7, the need for Christians to tie up their tongues. This is necessary because our tongues have the potential for much evil as well as much good. The tongue can stir up all sorts of commotion. Even in prayer it can offend, because we often pray with the wrong motive.

One's tongue is often a fairly good indicator of one's spiritual life. James has already referred to it as a "world of iniquity" (James 3:6). The tongue speaks what lies hidden in the heart. There is a lot more to be said about how much damage can be done by an unbridled tongue.

Christians are exhorted not to talk against other Christians, not to put them down. To do so is a verbal assault. Slanderous talk, defamation of character, and false accusations are gross evils and should never be committed by believers. The same is true even of what we might think of as minor offenses, like verbal pinpricks, "digs," jibes, and loud-mouthed abuse. When these are said with intent to injure, it is wrong.

Evil speaking is equivalent to judging other Christians. When we pass judgment upon other people's attitudes and actions, we are in a real sense claiming to be superior to the ones we criticize. By judging others, we imply that what we disapprove of in them is absent in us. We must be extraordinarily careful not to suggest that we know all the extenuating circumstances and can arrive at accurate conclusions about hidden motives. How arrogant, how braggadocious of us to do that!

Evil speaking is not only equivalent to judging. It is also against God's law. The definite article "the" does not appear in the Greek text. Therefore, we must be less than dogmatic about how we understand which law is referred to here. If it relates to the Mosaic law, then Leviticus 19:16 applies because this passage forbids tale-bearing. If the law refers to the law of love, as some believe, then Galatians 5:6 and 13–15 apply.

What we can be sure of in either case is that God's law is violated when Christians use their tongues in sinful ways against other Christians. The end result of such behavior makes the one doing it guilty of judging the law of God and indirectly judging God Himself.

It is bad enough to judge other Christians and even to criticize the law that forbids such judging, but it is worse still to sin against the God Who gave the law. Can you think of anything worse than finding fault with God? The very thought of such behavior is repulsive! God alone possesses the right to enforce His law and to deal as He pleases with those who violate it.

SINNING AGAINST GOD'S WILL

(James 4:13–17)

Human pride manifests itself in many ways. A haughty spirit, an air of superiority, an unforgiving spirit—such practices and more relate to pride. In fact, when you really think about it, there are few sins that cannot be traced to pride and selfishness.

Our pride shows up prominently in our spirit of independence. We must never, ever forget that we need to constantly be dependent upon God. It appears that some of the scattered Jews to whom James was writing were more dependent upon their own skills and wisdom than upon God. They had a considerable part in the business of the Roman Empire. Some of them were doubtless itinerant merchants who were making a lot of money and forgetting their need to keep God in their businesses. They were planning without consulting God. It takes planning ahead to not do that.

Keep in mind that James was not condemning these people for making money. Instead, he was pointing out that they were doing so without giving much thought to God, His work, and His will for them. The main concern of these Jews who were businessmen was to make more money, and in the process they left God out of their affairs. James was impatient with them.

Those who plan without God's direction, whether they are businessmen, homemakers, professionals, or others, thereby betray their egotism. They become self-confident. We all need to watch out for that trap which the devil sets before us. Planning without God is really foolish, because no one, however self-sufficient he is, can ascertain the future with certainty. Everything about life and earning a livelihood is transient. We are all just like "a vapor that appears for a little while and then vanishes away" (James 4:14).

Instead of doing their best to keep God in their businesses, James' audience (at least some of them) were busy "boasting" in their own ignorance. My, how far pride can take us. James says it clearly. Pride disparages others, ignores the Word of God, sets itself up as a critic of God's Word, reckons that self is fully adequate for any eventuality, lives independently of God, and as a final insult glories in itself. Committing all or even some of these sins is bad enough, but rejoicing and reveling in them is indeed the crowning act of sinful pride (4:16).

It seems that James had in mind some of his readers who would boast that they have not indulged in the sins he enumerated. To them he wrote scathing words: "Therefore to one who knows the right thing to do and does not do it, to him it is sin" (4:17).

What this means is that sins of omission are just as much sin as those of commission. Sin is missing the mark. Of course, whenever the right mark is missed, a wrong one is hit. Putting it another way, we sin when we practice evil or do evil things, but we also sin when we fail to do what we know God wants us to do.

All these words from James should alert us to our own imperfections and keep us from busying ourselves finding faults in others. Paul put it this way: "Brethren, even if anyone is caught in any trespass, you who are spiritual, restore such a one in a spirit of gentleness; each one looking to yourself, so that you too will not be tempted" (Galatians 6:1). To the Corinthian Christians he said: "But if we judged ourselves rightly, we would not be judged" (1 Corinthians 11:31). What all this boils down to is: let us keep a critical eye on ourselves and let God deal with all His servants and creatures as He pleases.

Some Expressions of Practical Atheism
- Criticizing others (James 4:11a)
- Ignoring God's law (James 4:11b)
- Opposing the Lawgiver (James 4:12)
- Sidestepping the Lord (James 4:15)

Some solid stepping stones for our journey:

(1) Self-examination

(2) A humble spirit

(3) A forgiving spirit

(4) Planning well with God's guidance

(5) Honoring God's Word and His will always

Did you find any other stepping stones in this passage?

(1)

(2)

(3)

11

THE MISUSE
OF MONEY

(JAMES 5:1–6)

How much money does it take to make a person rich? Put another way, how little does a person need to have to be classified as poor? I guess we would have to say, in response to both of these questions, that it pretty much depends on the financial position of the one answering the questions.

Regardless of how we respond to these questions, it is true, as someone said, that earthly possessions relate to four classes of people. First, there are those who are rich in earthly treasures but poor in heavenly assets. Second, some folks are poor in this world's goods but are rich with regard to God. Third, many are poor in both heavenly and earthly things. Fourth, a few Christians have much of this world's goods and are generous toward God and His work on earth and blessed with heavenly blessings.

Some Christians appear to have the impression that God is not pleased with people who are wealthy. This most certainly is not true. We only need to think about rich individuals whom God nevertheless used mightily: Abraham, Isaac, Amos, Joseph of Arimathaea, and Philemon are examples of this.

In 5:1–6, James deals with those who have plenty of this world's wealth, yet live in spiritual poverty. He also sets forth the cries of the employees and the crimes of the employer.

POVERTY WITH PLENTY
(James 5:1–3)

A farmer once went to listen to John Wesley's preaching. Wesley was treating the subject of money and developed it under three major divisions. His first point was "Get all you can." The old farmer nudged his neighbor and whispered, "This man has something worthwhile to say, that's good preaching."

Wesley's second point was "Save all you can." The farmer was really delighted to hear this coming from a man of God. "Was there ever anything like this?" he again whispered to his friend.

The famous preacher proceeded to denounce thriftlessness and waste, and the farmer rubbed his hands vigorously as he thought, "All of this have I been taught from my youth and up." This man thought salvation would come to his home if he kept on getting and hoarding.

Wesley's third point was not received too well by the farmer. His point was "Give all you can." The farmer responded with, "Oh, no, he's spoiled it again."

James seems to have in mind people, like the farmer in the story, who have their heaven in a bank instead of having their bank in heaven. We do live in a highly materialistic, money-minded age. Even believers can easily slip into the pitfalls that James describes. We can, and sometimes do, envy those with great wealth because we do not have much. James was not envying the wealthy in these verses, he was rebuking them.

There is some reason to question whether James was addressing wealthy Christians or non-Christian wealthy people with his words, "Come now, you rich" (James 5:1). If they were wealthy believers, they must not have been using their riches wisely. Alternatively, if non-Christians were the object, they must have been accumulating assets at the expense of the poorer believers who worked for them. Because James did not address his readers with the familiar phrase "brethren," which he uses in verse 7, there is substantial reason to believe that he was addressing non-Christians in the first six verses of James 5. Of course, even if this was the case, his words still apply to the believers who were not using their resources wisely. Barnabas, who was a wealthy Christian, sold his property and used the proceeds to help the poor (Acts 4:36–37). He serves, therefore, as a model for other Christians.

"Weep and howl" (James 5:1) indicates how dramatically the people of the East often expressed themselves. The word "howl" is used in Scripture only with regard to violent grief. The losses that the rich will suffer in the day of judgment are the cause of their woeful lamentations. James may have prophetically had the AD 70 destruction of Jerusalem in mind, as well as other judgments in the future.

In Bible times, there were three major sources of riches: foodstuffs, garments, and precious metals. James did not mention these three by name, but his description of the destruction of their riches includes all three of these assets. The language indicates that the foodstuffs had already begun to rot. Their riches were "rotted" (5:2) and their garments were moth-eaten (full of holes). The costly gold and silver had also begun to tarnish and rust. James' point is that everything the rich people had and continued to hoard was worthless as far as eternal rewards were concerned.

WRONGED WORKERS

(James 5:4–6)

A common and widespread complaint of many employees is that they are overworked and underpaid. Rarely do we hear of an employee who commends an employer for not giving him or her much to do and overpays him or her. Let's face it, pleasing some people is almost impossible. Many times, the more we get, the more we want. It is just human nature, it seems. But, on the other side of the coin, it is true that those who make a lot of money and have a lot of money often misuse those who work for them.

James was led by the Spirit of God to complain in strong words against the rich of his day for wrongs that they committed against both God and man (James 5:4–6). They sinned against God when they elevated themselves in pride. They sinned by trampling men and women underfoot in order to lift themselves up.

The rich defrauded the poor by withholding their earned wages. The rich employers were in such a mad quest to make more and more money that they cheated their employees. Those who owned fields of grain deprived those who cut and harvested the crop to such an extent that they got only the least possible, meager pay.

Just as the blood of Abel cried out (Genesis 4:10), so the deserved wages of those who harvested loudly cried out against the injustices of the landowners (James 5:4). In addition, those who were cheated cried out to God. Their prayers "reached the ears of the Lord of Sabaoth" (5:5). Who, we might ask, is the Lord of Sabaoth? He is the Lord of both heaven and earth. He marshals the hosts of heaven to the aid of His people on earth. He is the Guardian, the Leader, and the Protector of His own. God knows about the distress of His own and in His way and time He brings retribution.

The rich sometimes not only deprive their workers, but also revel in luxury at the expense of their misused employees. Calloused and conscienceless, they continue in extravagant self-indulgence. The rich to whom James is referring no more thought of the needs of others or of future judgment from God than animals have thought. These hoarders have fattened their hearts like animals fatten themselves without any concern for "the day of slaughter" (5:5).

All of us, Christian or non-Christian, have a tendency to indulge the flesh—to fulfill the desires common to humanity. The words of James ought to keep us on guard against embracing the materialistic philosophy of our generation and becoming earthly minded. Satan can, and all too often does, keep God's children so busy thinking how wonderful it would be to become rich that they forget their paychecks really belong to the Lord. The question is not "What would you do if you had a lot of money?" Rather, it is, "What do you do with money you now have?"

A final grievance completes the accusation James made against the uncaring and cruel rich. They "condemned and put to death the righteous man" (5:6). Following the example of Jesus, these Christians did not rise to insist upon their rights. They suffered in silence, counting it all joy that they could share Jesus' sufferings. They believed that God in His own time and way would vindicate the right and vanquish the wrong; and in assurance they gladly endured their afflictions. Surely, God gave them the strength and boldness to do that. May we follow in their steps on our journey.

Stepping stones for the journey:

(1) Realize that we are responsible for how we use the money God provides for us.

(2) Money and most of the things we can do with it are very temporal. They bring only temporary pleasure.

(3) Respond to mistreatment in a Christian way.

(4) Remember that God hears our prayers and He is not pleased when we are cheated out of what belongs to us.

(5) Being a Christian is not a life of ease.

Did you find any other stepping stones in this passage?

(1)

(2)

(3)

PATIENCE, PLEASE

(JAMES 5:7–12)

Some time after the historic Welsh revival, a group of Christians got together to hold what they called a "testimony meeting." Today we might call it a "sharing time." One young man stood up and said he was on the gospel ship going 50 knots an hour. Soon another got up and tried, with enthusiasm, to outdo the other man by saying he was going 70 knots an hour on the gospel ship. A little old lady quickly stood up and said, "These young men had better look out or they will blow up their boilers; I have been going it afoot for forty years."

The point this dear lady was trying to make was in order. In the Christian life, it is the long, hard pull that counts. The Christian journey is not a 50-yard dash. In the Christian journey, short-winded runners will not get very far. God wants cross-country runners who have extraordinary endurance. This, of course, is not in order to *become* Christians, but is because we *are* Christians. We have been born again.

James exhorted his readers about the need for patience, and he gave them examples, with whom his readers were familiar, of others who had trekked on the same journey and had already arrived home in heaven.

EXHORTATION TO PATIENCE
(James 5:7–9)

This exhortation follows on the heels of what the Lord's brother had just said about Christians being treated unfairly and even being put to death in some instances. He reminds those who experienced harsh and sinful treatment of their need to continue being patient. How long were they to keep on being patient? The answer is, "Until the coming of the Lord" (James 5:8). What did James mean by the coming of the Lord? He was referring to what the apostle called "the blessed hope" (Titus 2:13). Students of Scripture have called this hope the *imminent hope*. When something is imminent, it means it could take place at any moment. The thing that James encouraged his fellow Christian Jews to keep in their minds was that Jesus, his brother, promised to return for them.

This hope was to be their source of encouragement, patience, and strength even during hard and trying times. All of us need to have that same hope in our minds, looking forward to the return of Jesus Who will make right all the wrongs and take us to be with Himself. He may not come soon, but He *will* come, and we need to keep that promise and hope before us always.

James then gives the illustration of the farmer who waits and is patient for the rains to come so that his crops will produce an abundance. "The early and late rains" (James 5:7) refer to the two rainy seasons that occur annually in Palestine. The early rain came (and still comes) in October through November. The late rain comes in April through May.

There is no doubt about it: the first-century Christians believed that Jesus would come again in their lifetime. Most of those Christians did not understand the imminent return of Jesus to mean that they should simply fold their hands and wait. Maybe some did, but by no means everyone. All of us as Christians are to be busy about our Lord's business. We are told to work, because the night, the time of God's judgment after Jesus returns, is coming.

In the meantime, we Christians need to be patient and strengthen our hearts, because the "coming of the Lord is at hand" (5:8). That is, He could come at any time. The Greek verbs translated "coming" (5:8) and "standing" (5:9) are in the perfect tense. Thus, both of these verbs refer to action completed in the past and continuing on now. James believed in Jesus' return for His people even before he wrote his epistle. Also, Jesus as divine Judge began to stand before the door before James wrote about it. Furthermore, Jesus continues to stand there now. Jesus' return—his coming back—was imminent, in that it could have come at any time in New Testament times, and this is still true today.

For this reason, Christians then and now should be encouraged about Jesus' return. There is really no room or time for grumbling, griping, complaining, criticizing, and faultfinding. These kinds of activities accomplish little and are really not pleasing to God.

A Christian woman was whining about her hard lot in life and in her frustration said, "Oh, I wish I had never been made." A friend standing nearby overheard her and replied, "My dear friend, you are not yet made; you are only being made, and you are quarreling with God's processes." We should always realize that God often uses hardships and difficulties to conform us into the image of Jesus. When we insist on grouching and grumbling about how hard our life is and why God does not make it all better, we are really finding fault with God and acting as though He does not know what He is doing and is not in charge.

EXAMPLES OF PATIENCE

(James 5:10–12)

A characteristic feature of James' development is his frequent use of familiar subjects, objects, and illustrations and people: sea, wind, mirror, bridle, rudder, fruit, Abraham, Rahab, and Elijah. He has shown that the farmer exemplifies patience by waiting for the rains, not knowing for sure when they would come but knowing that they would come. In verses 10–12, James cites the prophets of old and Job as examples of real people who were patient amid the severest and most prolonged problems.

This reminds us how Jesus drew upon many natural things and happenings in His teaching ministry. Perhaps James learned this approach from his brother as he watched Him and listened to Him, even before he became Jesus' follower.

The prophets were divinely chosen to communicate God's truth to people. They fearlessly delivered whatever God told them to say. They were as hard on princes as they were on ordinary folks in their scathing denunciations of wickedness. Everyone alike came within the scope of their warnings, threats, counsels, calls to repentance, and promises, both publicly and privately. And, of course, the prophets were very unpopular with the non-Christians. Their reward for unflinching service to Jehovah-God was more persecution.

James wants his readers to emulate the prophets. How did they respond to their accusers, their hecklers? Those men of God of old were examples of suffering affliction and of patience, were they not? Indeed they were (5:10). For them, hardships were par for the course. Service for God meant they could expect to become the brunt of slander and the object of hatred. What's more, all who follow in their footsteps—speaking for God and warning sinners of threatening judgment—can anticipate the same results today.

Let's face it, the world is not a friend of grace. The opposition of the world to Christ has not lessened. In fact, each day the antagonism seems to intensify. The Christian who lives a godly life must expect to face opposition. The apostle Peter told his readers not to be surprised if they were subjected to the "fiery ordeal" (1 Peter 4:12). We are exhorted not to imagine, however, that Christians then and now did not or do not experience moments of defeat and despair. Observe the experiences of Jeremiah the prophet (Jeremiah 20:7–8) and Elijah the prophet (1 Kings 19:1–8). These are just two examples of the many who have gone before us who suffered for their faith while they were faithfully and steadfastly serving the Lord.

After James gives the illustration of the prophets as examples of great patience and confidence in God, he turns to Job as another example. Job's reactions to his most unusual and severe trials are remarkable. Without doubt, he is the proverbial paragon of patience. A glance at some of his attitudes toward his accusers and even his early protests against God makes us wonder whether he was as patient as James suggests.

We need to understand, however, that James used a word that implies strength, determination, and endurance to persist no matter what God sent to Job. James is not talking about exercising patience with irritating people. He calls attention to Job's steadfastness, a tenacity that prompted Job to declare, "Though he slay me, I will hope in him" (Job 13:15).

In the suffering of Job we see the "end," the purpose, of the Lord. The light afflictions work for us a far more exceeding and eternal weight of glory, while we look at things that are eternal (2 Corinthians 4:8–17). In other words, the problems and suffering we face now in this life are actually producing a valuable, eternal reward, as long as we keep our eyes on those eternal things. Job's great losses brought him to see God's majesty and greatness (Job 42:5–6). His afflictions caused him to appreciate more that God is of tender mercy even though He allows His own to suffer. The troubles that God permits to come our way are not without purpose.

God is not trying to be mean to us. He intends for us to emerge from the ordeals with a clearer concept of His unfailing mercies and compassion.

> ### Observe Some of God's Incentives for Patience
> - The Lord's Return
> - Precious fruit
> - The Judgment Seat
> - God's tender mercy

Stepping stones for the journey:

(1) Patience, even with those who do you wrong

(2) Endurance, as a good soldier

(3) Anticipation of the Lord's coming

(4) Avoidance of the sins of complaining, grumbling, getting even, feeling sorry for yourself

Did you find any other stepping stones in this passage?

(1)

(2)

(3)

13

PRAYER REALLY DOES WORK

(JAMES 5:13–20)

Four-year-old David had been tormenting his sister Caroline all afternoon. He was throwing small stones at her and a few of them actually hit her. That evening, while she was saying her prayers before getting into bed, Caroline asked God to bless David and please keep him from throwing stones and tormenting her. After she finished her prayer, she remembered that she had told God about the problem before, so she added, "And by the way, dear God, I've mentioned this to you several times before."

James closes his epistle with an encouragement to Christians to pray. He also lays down the prerequisites for getting a favorable response from God, Who truly does hear and answer prayer. Sometimes the answer is "yes"; sometimes it is "no"; and then sometimes He also answers with "wait."

For the Christian, prayer is communication with the Almighty God. Each and every believer has access to the throne of God. Everyone in His family can reach Him in an instant. The veil that separated the Holy Place from the Most Holy Place in the Old

Testament was torn open from the top to the bottom when Jesus arose from the dead.

Note the connection between what we said in Chapter 12 about Christians' need for patience as they endure mistreatment from those over them (James 5:7–12). James exhorts these same people to pray and praise God even as they endure hardship and misfortune.

THE PRACTICE OF PRAYER
(James 5:13–14)

James asked his readers to pray for any among them who were suffering or had trouble of some kind. The word "suffering" may be used to refer either to physical illness or mental illness such as depression. Because the same word is used in James 5:14 and is translated "sick," it appears that the description used in verse 13 refers to physical illness.

The praying that these folks were called upon to do involved continuous communication with God. Prayer was to be an ongoing exercise. Prayer may not always solve all our problems to our liking, but praying often does radically change our attitudes toward our problems. When the believer prays, he or she can receive God's sufficient grace to shoulder the burdens. Prayer is not something we can use to change God's mind. Rather, it helps us to see and understand God's mind.

Some of the people among James' readers were very likely "cheerful" (5:13). They were told to "sing praises" (presumably to God) for themselves or perhaps even for those who were suffering. The "sick," however, were instructed to "call for the elders of the church" to help them. These "elders" were the leaders of the assemblies. They were instructed to pray for the afflicted and anoint them with oil that had a therapeutic value. (Students of God's Word differ over what this anointing involved and whether elders should still do this today.)

It is important to recognize that James ascribes no healing power to the elders, and that the sick are not instructed to attend a mass healing campaign. The elders visited the home at the invitation of the sick person. The word translated "anointing" can also be rendered as "rubbing." In view of the fact that olives were plentiful and the oil from them was used as a medicine in Bible times, it seems that James instructed the elders to perform both a medical and a spiritual ministry. The reason elders applied the oil is that doctors in those days were scarce and expensive. Hence, it often fell to the church elders to serve both the physical and the spiritual needs of the flock.

Some think that this passage in James supports their view that some possess the gift of healing today. However, there is no warrant or basis for a claim that the elders who were called upon here to come to the aid of the sick had a gift of healing. The actual cause of the healing was not the olive oil, the gift of healing, or even the prayer of faith. Rather, James made it clear that "the Lord will raise him up" (5:15).

The "prayer of faith" does not refer to a special kind of prayer or a certain degree of faith. James, in keeping with the context, seems to be stressing the fact that in order for prayer to be acceptable and availing, it must be accompanied by faith in God, just like all other aspects of the Christian life.

Although the Bible does not teach that all physical ailments are the result of sin, James implies that some physical distresses may be traced to unconfessed sins (5:16).

THE PERSEVERANCE OF PRAYER

(James 5:17–20)

Many Christians feel ill at ease and inadequate in prayer. They view their temptations, weaknesses, and failures as peculiar to themselves alone. Some imagine that deeply spiritual, almost sinless, Christians are the only people who can pray the effectual fervent prayer. James reminded his Christian readers that Elijah prayed effectually and fervently, and he was no super-saint. In fact, he was beset by all of the temptations common to man. But his prayers had a certain quality about them that resulted in supernatural effects. This man, Elijah, prayed persistently and frequently.

God certainly used Elijah mightily. That should encourage other Christians, especially since Elijah "was a man with a nature like ours" (5:17). The point James is making here is that Elijah, celebrated though he was, suffered the same things and was subject to trials and weaknesses similar to those that others experience. The historic and inspired record of Elijah's life is in 1 Kings 17–19. It reveals that at times he stood on the mountaintop of victory and at other times he descended into Bunyan's valley of despair. By no means was he perfect, and James surely did not intend to present him as such. Still, Elijah, notwithstanding his faults, was a man of prayer, and we should be that also.

In the last two verses of the book of James, the brother of Jesus gives a final plea and implies that indeed it is possible for a Christian to wander from his or her original commitments and loyalty to Jesus. Nevertheless, thanks to our forgiving heavenly Father, "the effective prayer of a righteous man can accomplish much" (5:16). That prayer can be the means by which the wanderer is brought back. Each believer has a responsibility, not only to keep himself unspotted by the world,

but also to encourage and assist his other brothers and sisters in the
Lord to return to their first love.

The work of rescuing sinning Christians through prayer and
personal counsel has significant and far-reaching consequences. He
"will save his soul from death" (5:20). This probably refers to saving the
believer from the premature physical death that sometimes results from
persistent sin. The wanderer's sin will be forgiven and covered by the
shed blood of Jesus. He will be restored in the Christian assembly.

<u>Keys to Answered Prayer</u>
- Obedience (5:14)
- Faith (5:15)
- Cleansing (5:15b)
- Confession (5:16a)
- Intercession (5:16b)
- Fervency (5:16c)

Stepping stones for the journey:

(1) Fervent prayer

(2) Constant praise to God

(3) Restoration of fellow Christians who have erred

(4) Perseverance in the faith

Did you find any other stepping stones in this passage?

(1)

(2)

(3)

CONCLUSION

We have met one of Jesus' brothers as we have walked through the epistle that bears his name. James has given us a lot of food for thought. We have discovered some of the many solid stepping stones about which the Spirit of God led him to write. The epistle of James is one of the most practical books of the New Testament.

James has taught us how to view our earthly possessions and how to perform well under pressure. He has reminded us of our need to reflect on Scripture in our daily lives. We can keep from becoming snobbish if we heed his advice. Our faith will bear fruit when we put forth the effort to have it function with good works. Our tongues need to be controlled; they need to be bridled and kept from boasting about ourselves.

God would have us know the difference between heavenly wisdom and earthly wisdom and understand which is most important. Often we easily become self-centered, and James has taught us how to claim the victory in Christ. It shocked some of us to learn that if we are not careful, we can become practical atheists even while we extol our faith in the one and only true God. James has even reminded his readers, and in turn us, how to manage our money to the glory of God. He touched a sore spot with many of us when he stressed our need for patience, and he gave us Biblical examples of those who modeled patience. Finally, God through James has encouraged and exhorted us to a life of prayer.

Perhaps you will find it helpful to reflect further on the solid stepping stones that were pointed out. Have a blessed, profitable, and delightful journey with the Lord. Do not forget, as a child of God, you never walk alone!

ABOUT THE AUTHOR

Dr. Robert P. Lightner is Professor Emeritus and Adjunct Professor of Systematic Theology at Dallas Theological Seminary. Prior to this, he was a professor at Baptist Bible Seminary in Johnson, NY. He is the author of 23 books, including *Safe in the Arms of Jesus*, *The Last Days Handbook*, and *The Case for Total Inerrancy*. He has contributed to 17 other books, created or collaborated on Sunday school materials, and had articles printed in 22 Christian periodicals. He is a frequent speaker at churches and conferences.

Dr. Lightner planted churches in New York and Arkansas and has assisted churches as an interim pastor more than thirty times. His mission trips have taken him to Paraguay, Venezuela, and Peru. He has received awards for his accomplishments over four decades.

Dr. Lightner was educated at Baptist Bible Seminary, Dallas Theological Seminary, and Southern Methodist University. Dr. Lightner and his wife, Pearl, are both from the Lebanon, Pennsylvania area. They have three daughters—Nancy Shotts, Nadine Bracy, and Natalie Steitz—and fourteen grandchildren.

Also available from Grace Acres Press:

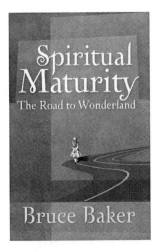

Spiritual Maturity:
The Road to Wonderland
by BRUCE BAKER
$19.95

"This is a layman's map providing directions for growing up in Christ."
—*Dr. Robert Lightner*
Dallas Theological Seminary

Resources and services for your organization available from Grace Acres Press:

- Author presentations
- Book excerpts for your newsletters
- Fundraising programs
- Writing seminars—elementary school through adults
- Publishing seminars and consulting
- Books, DVDs, and music CDs

Call today 888-700-GRACE (4722) or
visit our Web site: www.GraceAcresPress.com

CULTIVATING JOY

Also available from Grace Acres Press:

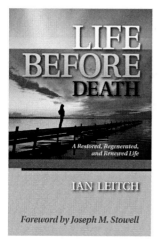

Life Before Death:
A Restored, Regenerated,
and Renewed Life
by IAN LEITCH
Foreword by JOSPEH M. STOWELL
$19.95

"Engaging, smart, persuasive, conver-
sational, and full of stories... Ian's book is
just like Ian. Enjoy!"

—Jerry B. Jenkins
Novelist

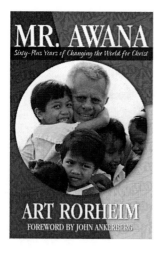

Mr. Awana:
Sixty-Plus Years of Changing
the World for Christ
by ART RORHEIM
Foreword by JOHN ANKERBERG
$19.95

"I know it will bless you..."

—Tony Evans
Author and pastor
Oak Cliff Bible Fellowship